Yvonne Müller

Collocation - A linguistic view and didactic aspects

Yvonne Müller

Collocation - A linguistic view and didactic aspects

GRIN Verlag

Bibliografische Information der Deutschen Nationalbibliothek: Die Deutsche Bibliothek verzeichnet diese Publikation in der Deutschen Nationalbibliografie; detaillierte bibliografische Daten sind im Internet über http://dnb.d-nb.de/ abrufbar.

1. Auflage 2008
Copyright © 2008 GRIN Verlag
http://www.grin.com/
Druck und Bindung: Books on Demand GmbH, Norderstedt Germany
ISBN 978-3-638-92049-0

UNIVERSITÄT PADERBORN
Die Universität der Informationsgesellschaft

Fakultät Kulturwissenschaften
Anglistik/Amerikanistik

Words in the Mind
WiSe 2007/08

Collocation

Number of words: 4718
Handed in: 30.01.2008

submitted by:

Yvonne Müller
LA Sek II (Englisch, Philosophie)
5. Sem.

Table of Contents

1 Introduction

The following paper deals with collocation. The topic is investigated with a linguistic view, but also didactic aspects should not be completely disregarded, because collocation is a very important topic especially for teachers. They have to know which word goes together with which term and how to explain these relationships to their pupils. The collocational aspect will have its meaning explained. Then a description of how collocations are used will follow. The third part of this paper presents Benson's understanding of collocation. He distinguishes between the collocations of different word classes. The first section is about lexical collocations, which contains collocations consisting of nouns, verbs, adverbs and adjectives. Then the most common lexical combinations will have their meaning explained. The first given type of collocation consists of verbs and nouns; the second one deals with the collocations of adjectives and nouns and the third section examines collocations of verbs and adverbs, while the last combination consists of adverbs and adjectives. These combinations are the most common lexical collocations, so others should be disregarded. The different kinds of collocations are examined concerning their behaviour in a sentence and the possibility they suggest to be substituted. After this examination the paper summarizes the structure of grammatical collocation. In the next part, Cowie's understanding of collocation is presented. He distinguishes between restricted and open collocations, which will be explained in this section. The next part of the paper contains some aspects one has to take account of when collocations are translated. Concerning translatability there are three different types of collocations: collocations of complete, partial and of no equivalence. These types are presented and examples are given. Finally, a few suggestions are given on how to teach collocation in school. Therefore, some different suggestions for teaching are given to make allowances for the student's age and advancement. The paper ends with a short summary and a final reflection.

2 Collocation

2.1 Meaning of Collocation

The term collocation, which has its origin in the Latin verb *collocare* (to arrage; to set in order), first appeared in the British linguist J.R. Firth's theory in 1951. He uses the term collocation to describe the co-occurrence of lexical items. Firth advocates the thesis that words get meaning from their collocates.

> Meaning by collocation is an abstraction at the syntagmatic level and is not directly concerned with the conceptual or idea approach to the meaning of words. One of the meanings of night is its collocability with dark.[1]

Collocation generally refers to the expression of words which are often used together such as *bitterly cold, rich imagination* or *close friends*. If you hear the first word, the second can be expected, or at least you can have an idea what it could be. In context with verbs and nouns collocation means the syntactic relationship between the verb and the noun phrase such as *to make a decision* or *to take a photo*. The words *make* and *decision* belong together in some way. They are collocates.

> For co-occurring in syntax we use the term **collocate**; an item collocates with another in its environment, the two together forming a **collocation**.[2]

To find collocates you take a word and look for other words which belong to the first, like in a mind-map. The word in the middle is called the *node*, its lexical behaviour is under examination[3]. The words around it are called *collocates,* as they occur in close proximity to the node[4]. In some cases collocates may be called equal partners and in some cases they may not. This can be attributed to the fact that one word out of the span can also be the node to the current node and the current node is also a collocate of that word. An example for equal partners is *pig* and *pork*. They can occur in one sentence. If you hear the word *pig* you can easily think of the word *pork* and if you hear the word *pork* you can easily think of the word *pig*. The word *pork* belongs to the set of the word *pig* and vice versa. Each of the words is used for a different range of collocates. If *pig* is the node you can also think of words like

[1] Firth, J.R. *Papers in Linguistics: 1934-1951*, (London: Oxford University Press, 1957), p. 196.
[2] Strang, B. M. H., *Modern English Structure*, 2nd edition. (London: Arnold, 1968), p. 224.
[3] Cf. Sinclair, John, *Corpus, Concordance, Collocation*. (Hong Kong: Oxford University Press, 1991), p. 175.
[4] Cf. Sinclair, John, *Corpus, Concordance, Collocation*. (Hong Kong: Oxford University Press, 1991), p. 170.

feed. Feed can be in the span of *pig*. But if you take *pork* as the node, *feed* will not be one of the first words one might think of. It is not used as frequently with *pork* as with *pig*. Even if there is a relationship between *pig* and *pork* they have ⌐different collocational ranges, and this establishes the fact that they belong to different lexical sets and are different lexical items.⌐[5] In a lexical set the lexical items have a similar range.[6] They might be synonyms or words with a similar meaning or use. In the example which is mentioned *sow* could be used to substitute for *pig* in many cases as they belong to the same lexical set. In the normal use of language they do not often occur together in one sentence because of their similar meaning. So even if pig and pork share some collocates, they do not form a collocation themselves.

Another aspect which is important for a collocation is a mutual expectation of both collocates.[7] If there are unequal partners one often has to speak about a free combination instead of a collocation. The combination *to write an essay* occurs together very often. The word *essay* occurs more often with *write* than vice versa. This is because there are more things to write than things one can do with an essay. Therefore, the term *to write an essay* is considered to be a free combination. As a rule one can say:

> [⌐] the more general a word is, the broader its collocational range; the more specific it is, the more restricted its collocational range.[8]

The classification of *to write an essay* is only caused by the inequality mentioned; not by the determiner as one might think of. Collocations can have words in between. If they contain a preposition or a grammatical structure they are regarded as grammatical collocations. This will be discussed in a later chapter.

> In English, as in other languages, there are many fixed, identifiable, non-idiomatic phrases and constructions. Such groups of words are called recurrent combinations, fixed combinations, or collocations. Collocations fall into two major groups: grammatical collocations and lexical collocations.[9]

Also grammatical collocations will have their meaning explained later, this paper focuses on lexical collocation; collocation between nouns, verbs, adjectives and adverbs.

[5] Catford, J. C., *A Linguistic Theory of Translation ⌐An Essay in Applied Linguistics*. (London: Oxford University Press, 1965), pp. 10-11f.
[6] Cf. Roos, Eckhard., *Kollokationsm⌐glichkeiten der Verben des Sehverm⌐gens im Deutschen und Englischen*. (Darmstadt: Lang 1975), p 13.
[7] Cf. Crystal, David. *The Cambridge Enciclopaedia of the English Language*. (Cambridge: Cambridge University Press, 1995), p. 162.
[8] Baker, Mona. *In Other Words. A Coursebook on translation*. (London: Routledge, 1992), p. 50.
[9] Benson, M.; Benson, E.; Ilson, R.. *The BBI Combinatory Dictionary of English. A Guide to Word Combinations*. (Amsterdam: John Benjamins Publishing Company, 1986), p. IX.

2.2 Use of Collocation

Collocations exist because of the use of language. This is an aspect which differs from person to person and so collocations do also. It starts with different associations which depend on one's job, mood, area, education, experience and so on. But like in language in general, collocations have special prevailing conditions as well. Different people only choose different words out of the collocates of a node. If you ask for an association of *pig* a hungry person may answer with *roast*, a farmer may answer with *pigsty* or *feed*, someone who has just visited a farm for the first time may say *stench* and so on. All these different words are collocates of *pig*; they are in the collocational range of the node *pig*.

> To sum up, we create new collocations all the time, either by extending an existing range or by deliberately putting together words from different or opposing ranges.[10]

If one hears a new combination for the first time, one may find it strange, like a violation of the rules of collocation. Everyone will be understood if he or she violates collocational preferences as long as the content makes sense for example saying *I have already made my homework.* The sentence will stand out as awkward and the speaker is identified as a foreign language speaker. This is because collocations differ from language to language and there is no reason for a special combination.

> Why do builders not *produce* a building or authors not *invent* a novel, since they do invent stories and plots? No reason as far as dictionary definitions of words are concerned. We don't say it because we don't say it.[11]

The reason for the necessity of teaching collocations to second language learners is that first language learners have plenty of opportunity to take collocations out of usage. The thing which is completely natural for first language learners needs special attention for second language learners. Therefore, there will be a brief chapter about teaching collocation in school later in this paper.

[10] Baker, Mona. *In Other Words. A Coursebook on translation.* (London: Routledge, 1992), p. 52.
[11] Bolinger, D. and Sears, D.. Aspects of Language. (New York: Harcourt Brace Javanovich, 1981), p. 55.

3 Benson's Understanding of Collocation

3.1 Lexical Collocations

3.1.1 Definition of Lexical Collocations

The first theory of collocation which should be presented is Benson's, even if it is not the first chronologically. Benson's theory is the one which is examined most detailed and given first because its classification is the strongest and should be the basis with which other theories can be compared. Collocations can consist of words belonging to different word classes. First, all possible combinations are given; but the more detailed examination is restricted to the following syntactic patterns which are regarded as the most common ones.[12] Benson classified collocations into two groups; lexical and grammatical collocations. Lexical collocations consist of nouns, adjectives, verbs and adverbs. They normally do not contain prepositions, infinitives or clauses, while grammatical collocations embrace this.

> A grammatical collocation, in contrast to a lexical collocation, is a phrase that consists of a noun, an adjective, or a verb plus a preposition or grammatical structure such as an infinitive or clause (Benson et al., 1986).[13]

Lexical collocations usually not only appear in one sentence but often their positions are right next to each other. If a more detailed explanation or specification is given to one of the collocates there can be words in between them. The distance in which the node and its collocate appear in a sentence is called the span. "A span of -4, +4 means that four words on either side of the node (q.v.) word will be taken to be its relevant verbal environment."[14] An example is: *The dog which wanted to run without his lead started to bark.* The words *dog* and *bark* are collocates; even if there are nine words between them. In collocations of different word classes are differences in the possible and most frequent size of the span. Even if this paper only examines the four most frequently used combinations there are seven possible combinations.

---

[12] Cf. Irsula Pena, Jesús Ismael. *Substantiv – Verb – Kollokationen.* (Leipzig: Universitätsverlag, 1992), p. 56.

[13] Benson, Morton; Benson, Evelyn; Ilson, Robert. *The BBI Combinatory Dictionary of English. A Guide to Word Combinations.* (Amsterdam: John Benjamins Publishing Company, 1986), p. IX.

[14] Cf. Sinclair, John, *Corpus, Concordance, Collocation.* (Hong Kong: Oxford University Press, 1991), p. 175.

L1: verb (which means creation/action) + noun/pronoun/prepositional phrase e.g. *come to an agreement, launch a missile*

L2: verb (which means eradication/cancellation) + noun e.g. *reject an appeal, crush resistance*

L3: [adjective + noun] or [noun used in an attributive way + noun] e.g. *strong tea, a crushing defeat, house arrest, land reform*

L4: noun + verb naming the activity which is performed by a designate of this noun e.g. *bombs explode, bees sting*

L5: quantifier + noun e.g. a swarm of bees, a piece of advice

L6: adverb + adjective e.g. hopelessly addicted, sound asleep

L7: verb + adverb e.g. argue heatedly, apologize humbly.[15]

3.1.2 Collocations between Verbs and Nouns

Collocations between verbs and nouns are often fixed expressions. That means the synonymy of both collocates is restricted. The verb in the combination *to commit murder* can be substituted with the verb *to perpetrate*, but the new combination seems to be the only combination which is possible and is not used frequently. Another example shows that the synonymy of nouns is also restricted. One can say *hold a funeral*, but not **hold a burial.*[16] In this example the two collocates are separated by a determiner; the span can be enlarged even more with a description of the funeral, etc.. Even if this is the case, the restrictions of the expected collocate do not change. Hence, the collocates of a verb □ noun collocation can occur within a relatively large span.

[15] Cf. Matgorzata Martyńska. Do English language learners know collocations? Investigationes Linguisticae vol. IX Poznan, (2004).
[16] Benson, Morton; Benson, Evelyn; Ilson, Robert. *Lexicographic Description in English.* (Amsterdam: John Benjamins Publishing Company, 1986), pp. 258-259.

9

3.1.3 Collocations between Adjectives and Nouns

The collocates of an adjective □noun collocation usually occur right next to each other. Even if there is an order in which adjectives appear, the collocation is seldom separated. The adjective describes the noun directly and therefore, its position is in front of the noun. An example is *close friends* or *rich imagination*. If more detailed information should be added to one of the nouns, it occurs in front of the whole collocation.

Like the verb □noun collocation the adjective □noun collocations seems to have a restricted replaceability of the collocates with synonyms. For example one can say *a rich imagination*, but not *a wealthy imagination*.

3.1.4 Collocations between Verbs and Adverbs

Verbs are usually described or specified with an adverb. This combination occurs in a sentence, but like in the verb □noun collocation the span can be enlarged by other words. The collocation in the sentence *He is affected deeply* cannot be separated by a by-agent, but their order can be changed, which is the most common solution. Three different word orders are possible, but most speakers would prefer to use the last possibility.

He is affected by her death deeply.

He is affected deeply by her death.

He is deeply affected by her death.

Again the synonymy of both collocates is restricted. One can say *affected deeply*, but one would not say *deeply upset*. Even if *upset* can be regarded as a synonym, one would prefer to say *extremely upset*. Nevertheless there are examples in which collocates can be substituted by synonyms, one example is *deeply hurt*.

3.1.5 Collocations between Adverbs and Adjectives

Collocations between adverbs and adjectives usually do not have any words in between. The adverb describes the adjective and therefore its position is right in front of it like in the example *bitterly cold*. The span of adverb □adjective collocations is usually small.

The use of synonyms for a collocate is restricted. Adverbs like *extremely* can go together with *cold*, but one cannot use a synonym of/ for (?) *bitterly* like *plainly* or *hardly* in front of *cold*. Also substituting the word *cold* with *frosty* or *chilly* would lead to an unusual combination.

3.2 Grammatical Collocations

Grammatical collocations consist of nouns, verbs, adverbs or adjectives in combinations with a grammatical feature like a clause. In contrast to lexical collocations they can also contain a preposition or an infinitive.

> Collocations in which two lexical elements co-occur are called □lexical collocations□, collocations in which a lexical and a more grammatical element (such as a preposition) co-occur, are called □grammatical collocations□.[17]

Examples for grammatical collocations are *advantage over, to be afraid that, by accident*, etc.. Chomsky gives the following example of a grammatical collocation (which is called *a close construction* in Chomsky□s terminology): *decide on a boat*, meaning □choose (to buy) a boat□ but on the other hand, *decide on a boat*, meaning □make a decision while on a boat□is a free combination (*a loose association* in Chomsky□s terminology).[18] Native speakers of English feel that the components of *decide on* collocate with each other, and they will most likely reject violations of collocability such as *decide at a boat.*

---

[17] Nesselhauf, Nadja. *Collocations in a Learner Corpus.* (Amsterdam: John Benjamins Publishing Company, 2005), p. 21.
[18] Chomsky, Noam. *Aspects of the theory of syntax.* (Cambridge: M.I.T. Press, 1965), p. 191.

As it is the case with lexical collocations, there are also different types of grammatical collocations. The first category consists of the main word (a noun, an adjective, a verb) plus a preposition or ⌐to+infinitive☐or ⌐that-clause☐and is characterized by eight basic types of collocations:

G1: noun + preposition e.g. *blockade against, apathy towards*

G2: noun + to-infinitive e.g. *He was a fool to do it, They felt a need to do it*

G3: noun + that-clause e.g. *We reached an agreement that she would represent us in court, He took an oath that he would do his duty.*

G4: preposition + noun e.g. *by accident, in agony*

G5: adjective + preposition e.g. *fond of children, hungry for news*

G6: adjective + to-infinitive e.g. *it was necessary to work, it☐s nice to be here*

G7: adjective + that-clause e.g. *she was afraid that she would fail, it was imperative that I be here*

G8: 19 different verb patterns in English e.g. verb + to-infinitive (*they began to speak*), verb + bare infinitive *(we must work)* and other.[19]

4   Cowie☐ Understanding of Collocation

This classification, made by Benson, is not the only way to distinguish different kinds of collocations. Cowie☐s definition of a collocation, formulated a few years before Benson☐s, does not differ fundamentally from Benson☐s. He defines a collocation as a co-occurrence of two or more lexical items as realizations of structural elements within a given syntactic pattern.[20] Cowie differentiates between pure idioms, figurative idioms, restricted collocations and open collocations. There is no distinction between lexical and grammatical collocations, but it is differentiated between collocations which contain two main elements and

[19] Cf. Matgorzata Martyńska. ☐Do English language learners know collocations?☐Investigationes Linguisticae vol. IX Poznan, (2004).
[20] Cf. Cowie, A. P. ☐The place of illustrative material and collocations in the design of a learner☐s dictionary☐ Stevens, P. ed. In Honour of A.S. Hornby. (Oxford: Oxford University Press, 1978), p. 132.

collocations which contain only one main element. Open collocations are free combinations of two meaningful elements e.g. a *broken window*. Every part of this open collocation kept its usual meaning and therefore, they are free combinable. In a restricted collocation only one part keeps its usual meaning. In the example *jog one's memory* the word *jog* is not used in the way it usually is.

> Cowie's classification, which was also adopted by Howarth, was probably inspired by Aisenstein (1979), who makes a similar distinction between verbs with a "secondary, abstract meaning", verbs with a grammaticalized, wide and vague meaning and verbs with a "very narrow and specific meaning"[21]

Cowie distinguishes in terms of how combinable the constituents of a collocation are. The more combinable a word is, the greater its chance to be classified as an open collocation. A later definition, given in 1981, clarifies his criteria further.

> A collocation is by definition a composite unit which permits the substitutability of items for at least one of its constituent elements (the sense of the other element, or elements, remaining constant)[22]

5 Translatability of Collocations

Collocations often differ from language to language. While it is *to do one's homework* in English, it is *Hausaufgaben machen* in German. *To make one's homework* sounds as strange in English as *Hausaufgaben tun* in German. Therefore, one has to translate a collocation as a whole expression and not word by word.

> If we take into account the fact that expressions in context not only have conceptual meanings but also convey connotative, stylistic, affective, reflected, and collocative meanings, it will in fact be difficult to discover any pair of expressions in actual speech which are really equivalent.[23]

A synonymous expression in the target language has to be found. While translating one has to take account of the overall meaning, even if this means changing the vocabulary. Collocations

[21] Nesselhauf, Nadja. *Collocations in a Learner Corpus*. (Amsterdam: John Benjamins Publishing Company, 2005), p. 22.
[22] Cowie, A. P. "The treatment of collocations and idioms in learners' dictionaries" in: Applied linguistics 2, 1981. P 224.
[23] Van den Broeck, R. (1978) "The Concept of Equivalence in Translation Theory: Some Critical Reflections" in: Holmes, J., Lambert, J. & Van den Broeck, R. (eds.) Literature and Translation: New Perspectives in Literary Translation, Leuven: acco. p. 36

are not idiomatic, but describe facts, objects or phenomenon of reality.[24] So they are usually not expressed by totally different words in the other language. At least one collocate of the source language must not be changed when translated to the target language. This part of the collocation acts like a basis; therefore, it consists of the more important collocate. There are only a few exceptions to this rule; these exceptions, collocations with zero equivalence, are introduced later.

If a collocation is not known by the translator, he or she may translate it word by word. The consequence is a wrong, or at least a strange translation. As a result of this, the translator is identified as a foreign language speaker. To avoid these errors it is important for translators to improve their knowledge of collocation permanently.[25] Therefore, the translator has to know the different types of equivalence. The three types: complete equivalence, partial equivalence and no equivalence are presented now.

5.1 Complete Equivalence

Complete equivalent collocations consist of components which do not show any differences when they are translated from the source language to the target language.

> This implies complete correspondence between words and expressions in two languages as regards to content and register.[26]

These combinations can be translated word by word. Examples for German-English translation are given below:

unexpected discovery = *unerwartete Entdeckung*

rancid butter = *ranzige Butter*

throw a shadow = *einen Schatten werfen*

to take something seriously = *etwas ernst nehmen*

[24] Cf. Irsula Pen, Jesús Ismael. *Substantiv Verb Kollokationen.* (Leibzig: Universitätsverlag, 1992), p. 51.
[25] Cf. *ibid.* p. 154.
[26] Svensén, Bo. *Practical Lexicography. Principles and Methods of Dictionary-Making.* (Oxford: Oxford University Press, 1993), p.143.

These examples show that all types of collocations, classified in an earlier chapter, can be translated with their full equivalent. There is no way to distinguish between the types of equivalence by only knowing the collocation of one language.

5.2 Partial Equivalence

Most collocations show a partial equivalence when they are translated. That means there is ⸢incomplete agreement of the content and register of the words in the respective languages⸣[27]. Therefore, one of the collocates, of the source language must not be changed when translated to the target language, but the other one has to be changed. One part of the collocation acts like a basis; therefore, it consists of the more important collocate; the one which is not changed. This importance is not attributed to one item because of its word class, but because of its meaning. Examples are:

heavy smoker = starker (= 'strong') Raucher

feverish condition = fieberhafte Erkrankung (='illness').

to fall ill = krank werden (= ⸢become⸣)

to lay/ set the table = den Tisch decken (= ⸢spread; cover⸣)

Collocations with collocates of every word class can be of partial equivalence; but however the case with full equivalent collocations one cannot distinguish them from another type of equivalence.

5.3 No Equivalence

Finally, no equivalence means that neither of the two elements of the collocations can be literally translated. Examples of no equivalence include idioms, endocentric compounds as well as structurally incongruent collocations. These collocations do not occur very often in German-English translation. There are some examples for single words denoting culture-

---

[27] Cf. *ibid.* p. 143.

specific concepts, like the German word *Kn☐del* or the English term *Lord Chancellor*[28]. An example for a collocational term is:

red tape = B☐rokratie

6 Teaching of Collocation

Collocations have to be taught in school. This needs special attention because there are a lot of collocations in the English language which are different than in German or other languages. These differences are one of the greatest sources of error. The most common example, which is taught very early in school, is the difference between *to do* and *to make*. So this should serve as an example. First, the teacher should clarify what the verbs express, so the pupils know when to use the verb. Then he or she should list the most important expressions, possibly each with a mind map. The teacher should avoid translating words, so that the pupils do not start to think in German or in their language. Instead of translations he or she can work with pictures, gestures, explanations or with the context. Context is very effective because collocations, like other words, get their meaning because of their use, in context.[29] It can be practised with texts, in which the pupils have to fill in the gaps. In general there are lots of other ways to teach collocational terms. Three ways will be quickly introduced. The first technique is ☐word fields☐ Here the collocations are taught with mind maps, so that the pupils can easily associate the words, because they link them with other already known words in their brain[30]. A second method is teaching with ☐antonyms☐ so that the learners can compare the verbs. The third way is teaching with ☐collocation quizzes☐ where the pupils see some nouns on the left and some verbs on the right, and have to make possible combinations. The teacher should use multisensory activities to take into consideration the different kinds of learners. He or she should at least work with the written words, his or her voice and pictures. But because collocations have much to do with use and repetition the pupils should also repeat the collocations and form sentences on their own.

---

[28] Cf. *ibid.* p. 145.
[29] Cf. Chomsky, Noam, *Syntactic Structures.* (The Hague: Mouton, 1972), p. 104.
[30] Cf. Spada, N.; Lightbown, P. M. ☐Second Language Acquisition☐ Schmitt, Norbert, ed. An Introduction to Applied Linguistics. (London: Arnold, 2002), p. 120.

16

7 Conclusion

This paper begins with an examination of collocation concerning its meaning and use. Collocation describes the syntactical co-occurrences of words. These are fixed, identifiable, non-idiomatic phrases and constructions. They consist of two or more lexical items which are used together more frequently than other combinations of words. This frequency causes a detailed examination of their structure. Therefore, collocations are classified. There are different ways to classify them; two possibilities were presented in this paper. The first way is Benson's who separated lexical and grammatical collocations. Lexical collocations consist of nouns, verbs, adverbs and adjectives, while grammatical collocations also include prepositions, that-clauses, infinitives and other grammatical items. As a result of his examination he distinguishes between seven lexical and eight grammatical combinations. Each part of these combinations is regarded as an equal, meaning-carrying item. Cowie, who's theory is presented after Benson's, differentiate between collocations in which all parts carry an equal amount of meaning and collocations with parts which carry more and parts which carry less of its original meaning. The first kind of collocation is called open and the second one restricted. The section after the presentation of these theories is about translatability of collocations. It was already said that collocations are non-idiomatic, fixed expressions; that means, the meaning of collocations can be concluded from the meaning of the items but nevertheless the items belong together. Therefore, collocations cannot always be translated word by word. Finally, the necessity of teaching collocation to second language learners is explained and a few suggestions how to teach collocation are given. Collocation should be taught in school because otherwise second language learners translate the collocation of their mother language into the target language. This cannot be done for the reasons explained in the section about translatability.

List of References

Baker, Mona. In *Other Words. A Coursebook on translation.* London: Routledge, 1992.

Benson, Morton; Benson, Evelyn; Ilson, Robert. *The BBI Combinatory Dictionary of English. A Guide to Word Combinations.* Amsterdam: John Benjamins Publishing Company, 1986.

Benson, Morton; Benson, Evelyn; Ilson, Robert. *Lexicographic Description in English.* Amsterdam: John Benjamins Publishing Company, 1986.

Bolinger , D.; Sears, D.. *Aspects of Language.* New York: Harcourt Brace Javanovich, 1981 (1968).

Catford, J. C., *A Linguistic Theory of Translation An Essay in Applied Linguistics.* London: Oxford University Press, 1965.

Chomsky, Noam. *Aspects of the Theory of Syntax.* Cambridge: M.I.T. Press, 1965.

Chomsky, Noam, *Syntactic Structures.* The Hague: Mouton, 1972.

Cowie, A. P. The place of illustrative material and collocations in the design of a learner's dictionary Stevens, P. ed. In Honour of A.S. Hornby. Oxford: Oxford University Press, 1978. Pp. 127-139.

Cowie, A. P. The treatment of collocations and idioms in learners dictionaries In: Applied linguistics 2, 1981. Pp 223-235.

Crystal, David. *The Cambridge Encyclopedia of the English Language.* Cambridge: Cambridge University Press, 1995.

Firth, J.R. *Papers in Linguistics: 1934-1951,* London: Oxford University Press. 1957.

Irsula Pen Jes s Ismael. *Substantiv Verb Kollokationen.* Leipzig: Universit tsverlag, 1992.

Matgorzata Martyńska. Do English language learners know collocations? Investigationes Linguisticae vol. IX Poznan, 2004.
http://www.staff.amu.edu.pl/~inveling/pdf/malgorzata_martynska_inve11.pdf

Nesselhauf, Nadja. *Collocations in a Learner Corpus.* Amsterdam: John Benjamins Publishing Company, 2005.

Roos, Eckhard, *Kollokationsm glichkeiten der Verben des Sehverm gens im Deutschen und Englischen.* Darmstadt: Lang, 1975.

Sinclair, John, *Corpus, Concordance, Collocation.* Hong Kong: Oxford University Press, 1991.

Spada, N.; Lightbown, P. M. Second Language Acquisition Schmitt, Norbert, ed. An Introduction to Applied Linguistics. London: Arnold, 2002.

Strang, B. M. H., *Modern English Structure,* 2nd edition. London: Arnold, 1968.
Svens n, Bo. *Practical Lexicography. Principles and Methods of Dictionary-Making.* Oxford:

Oxford University Press, 1993.

Van den Broeck, R. ⌐The Concept of Equivalence in Translation Theory: Some Critical Reflections⌐ in: Holmes, J., Lambert, J. & Van den Broeck, R. (eds.) Literature and   Translation: New Perspectives in Literary Translation, Leuven: acco, 1978.

CPSIA information can be obtained
at www.ICGtesting.com
Printed in the USA
LVIC031032040112

262362LV00001B